We Were There Too

Renee' Picardi

02/18/2011 19:08

ISBN 978-1-957582-50-4 (paperback)
ISBN 978-1-957582-51-1 (eBook)

Printed in the United States of America

Dedicated to my Best Forever Friend, my husband of 42 years, Pete. You take me wherever I want to go and give me everything I need and want. After 6 years of full time RVing I'm the happiest woman alive. May 2014

The cover photo was taken on a catamaran tour of the Napoli Coast, Kauai, Hawaii

09/17/2011

September 7, 2008
Hi Everyone,
We finally went to Chocolate World, PA and, of course, had a great time. When we first got there we walked into a huge room that was filled with rows and rows and displays of all our favorite candy in all types of containers and packages. We felt like kids wandering around trying to decide what to get. We didn't want to lug a lot of candy around all day and it was too hot to put chocolate in a 100 degree car, so we bought 1 bar each (Mounds) and ate it then and there and decided to come back later (which we didn't).

We then went on the factory tour, which was pretty interesting. It told of the life of Milton Hershey, the founder, and his wife and how he started the business. After about 6 failed chocolate stores he finally became so successful that after his wife died he built a school for orphaned under-privileged boys, and paid for their housing and college. Then he built the town so they would be able to support themselves. He left all his money to them to the tune of $60,000,000, (a lot of money in the 1950's) because he and his wife could not have children. The tour ended by showing where the cocoa beans came from, how the chocolate is made, how they use local cow's milk and sugar and the different types of bars they make. A machine counted out the thousands of Kisses, KitKats, Reese's Peanut Butter Cups and other candies that were being made right at that minute. Amazing!!! We then had our picture taken and put on 1 pound Hershey's chocolate bar labels and sent them to some friends and family for birthday gifts. It was neat. For lunch, I had a hot fudge chocolate sundae with Reese's Peanut Butter Cups as a topping, whipped cream and a cherry. Mmmmmm! We took home only two 1 pound plain milk chocolate bars. What a sugar high. We didn't go to the amusement park, as we both don't go on the rides, but we heard they were great.

A few days later we went to the Pennsylvania Renaissance Fair. We had a pretty, clear day. It was exciting to see all the costumes from Queen Elizabeth's day (1500's). A lot of the people that were visiting the fair came dressed in costumes too and received a discount on their ticket and, of course, there were a lot of actors and actresses dressed up and walking around. The shops were designed for the period in Old English Tudor and there were street vendors selling jewelry, fans, knives, swords, masks, puppets and all kinds of food. There was also free wine tasting from Hope Winery on the premises, and they had a very interesting store.

We watched a chess game played with real people dressed as the chess pieces on an open field and two ladies were calling out the moves. When a piece met another piece, all the other pieces left the grounds and the two pieces would have to do battle (using weapons from that time period such as swords, ball & chains, axes, etc) and the winner would stay on the field while the rest of the pieces would come back to the grounds to finish the game. The loser was carried off in a stretcher. This was done while the Queen and her ladies and entourage watched. We saw an amazing Archer demonstrate his skills and a joust tournament in which one of the ladies was kidnapped and almost burned at the stake. A knight on horseback saved her, thank goodness. There were so many activities and things to do and see. It was a perfect day.

When we were watching the end of the play where the Knight was married to the Lady by the Queen, I felt something crawling on me and I was feeling little pinpricks in my neck and shoulder. I couldn't find the thing at first, and when I finally felt it with my fingers I flung it away form me and I didn't know what it was. Later, Google told me it must have been a caterpillar that left little tiny spinney hairs in my skin from the back of my neck under my hair, across my shoulder to my chest and under my chin. I was a mess. Pete had to put duct tape on my neck and then quickly pull it off to get the spines out of my skin. Needless to say, I developed an itchy rash. We used alcohol, Calamine lotion, cortisone cream, aloe lotion and Aveeno. We tried everything, so we consulted a CVS pharmacist. Thank God I had some Prednisone for my Asthma. I used it for 5 days and now it is almost gone. So, don't sit under any trees in PA.

We traveled to the Gateway of Cape Cod Resort in Massachusetts. We met our son Joe and his new wife Joan there. We also met tropical storms Gustave and Hannah there too. We had heavy rain Friday night, most of the day on Saturday and a lot on Saturday night. That didn't stop us from having a good time. We looked at over 1,000 pictures of Joe & Joe's wedding on 8/8/08. We went to dinner on Saturday night (Lobster Scampi for me). It was a beautiful day on Sunday and we went sightseeing to a town called Sandwich on the Cape. We were going to have sandwiches in Sandwich (ha ha), but instead we had ice cream sundaes for lunch that were buy one get one free. WOW. We then visited a glass blowing museum. A young girl demonstrated how it was done and the end result was a pitcher. Very interesting. From there we visited a Grist Mill that used to ground corn into meal and saw the oldest house in New England (built in 1609), which was in the Hoxie family until the 1950's when it was donated as a museum. Do you believe people in that time period were taxed for the amount of stairs they had going to the second floor? That's why they built the stairs so steep. They were also taxed on the amount of windows in the house and all the metal they used. No wonder they had a revolution. We saw the Cape Cod Canal and wound up at a lobster bar. Joan taught Pete how to eat a whole lobster (including the head) while Joe and I watched. I like broiled lobster tails, but this was boiled whole. Not my cup of tea. It was a little too messy for my taste. I had shrimp and corn on the cob. We had so much fun and laughed a lot, but then I cried to see them go, because we won't see them again until Thanksgiving! That's too long not to see your kids, but we all have our own lives now and the time will go fast. Now it's back to PA to see Mike our son, and Pete's sisters Connie and Miggs before we leave for the south. We can't wait to go, but it's sad too.

Love to all,
Renee' and Pete

February 14, 2009

Hi Everyone,

After a very nice stay in warm and sunny Casa Grande, AZ we picked up Joe & Joan and Elsie and Alex (Joan's Mom & Dad) and dropped them off in Sedona, AZ at their condo time-share. We stayed at a campsite in Verde Valley. The elevation is more than 3,000 feet and it was a little chilly at night, (in the low 20's) but in the low 60's during the day. It was so nice to see everyone again.

Sedona is a beautiful city surrounded by huge red rock mountains and various shops and restaurants. There are some rock formations that have names, like Snoopy, Coffee Pot and Bell. Near the very beautiful Chapel of the Holy Cross are the Madonna and Child rock formation. We had to use our imagination a little to distinguish it, like when we are looking at clouds. I wouldn't have found any of these formations unless we had our little tour book, but it was lots of fun trying to figure them out. The Chapel is very small and rustic. Behind the alter are wall-to-ceiling glass windows that have a magnificent panorama of the surrounding red hills. It also has a lovely gift store and I picked out a gift for Gabrielle who is making her First Communion. We also drove around to find some of the areas that are supposed to rejuvenate you because of the force field coming up from underground. If we tried very hard and closed our eyes, we might have felt something (or did we imagine it). I'm not sure.

On Thursday afternoon we traveled to the Grand Canyon. It took us 2 hours to get there taking the scenic route (which was well worth it) cutting through mountains that were so beautiful we had to stop to take pictures. When we finally got to the Grand Canyon, it was late in the afternoon and the Canyon was shadowed with purple, blue and brown. The small white area at the bottom of the Canyon is the Colorado River, responsible for making the Canyon over thousands of years. It was still magnificent to look at. We took lots of pictures. Then the sun started to set. And Holy Crow! The whole Canyon was highlighted with gold. Then we took lots more pictures. Then OMG (oh my God) the sunset was amazing. We had to stop in the middle of the road and take more pictures. The clouds were alight with pink & blue and the gold in the sunset looked liquid. I have never seen anything like this before. We were so sorry when the sun finally set and it got dark pretty quick and the temperature plummeted. Going home through the mountains was exciting, because the road is so narrow and there are no lights on the road. But, the lights from the city, far away was awesome against the black background.

11

On Saturday, February 7, Joe, Joan & Elsie ran a marathon for charity. A marathon is 26.2 miles and takes about 5 hours to run. Joan ran a half marathon (13 miles and 2 ½ hours) and came in around 200 out of 500 runners, which was an impressive effort. Elsie came in 6th in her age group in a 3-mile run, around 40 runners. Joe ran with Elsie and when she finished, he caught up with Joan and finished the race with her. I was pretty impressed with their performance especially with the elevation and the course was up and down the hills. I walked from the car in the parking lot to their second floor condo and I was winded. I took pictures from their room's balcony. Overall, there were over 1,000 runners.

All too quickly it was Sunday and time for them to leave. It was J & J's sixth-month Anniversary and we saw a rainbow that reminded us of the rainbow on their wedding day. On the way back to Phoenix airport, we stopped off at a Casino (didn't win) and Montezuma's Castle. Tourists were not allowed to tour inside it as it is built in the side of the mountain and crumbling from age. It was a little bit of a letdown but the visitor's center showed us drawings of how it originally looked and all the information about the Indians that inhabited it. All in all we had a wonderful time together. After dinner, it was airport time and they all arrived home safe and sound.

Now we are in Apache Junction, AZ until Wednesday, February. 18. We decided to go to Palm Springs, CA and tour around that area. We'll keep in touch. Have a wonderful Valentine's Day.
Love to all,
Renee' & Pete

April 16, 2009
Hi Everyone,
Let me go back about 3 weeks to when we were in Palm Springs. Although it is very beautiful with Palm Trees everywhere and temps in the 80's, the air is so dry our skin felt leathery and was chafed white. We were constantly putting lotion on. Also, there is a fine dust everywhere and the winds gusting up to 55 mph kept us inside on more than one day. The dust gets inside the motor home somehow and I had to vacuum the runners of the windows and wipe everything down. Add the air pollution coming from Los Angeles and it is not the healthiest spot in the world. Needless to say, I got an URI.

While we were in Palm Springs we went to Indian Canyon where we mostly drove around the area. It was interesting to see some oases that were fed by underground springs and a creek. Like, right in the middle of nowhere there were groves of green Palm Trees. There was also a waterfall, but Pete had to hike about a mile just to get some movies of it. I passed on that and waited in the car with the air conditioner on. The Cahuilla Indians lived there many years ago, and although they don't live there anymore, it is still owned and run by that tribe.

The highlight of Palm Springs was an exciting and amazing Aerial Tramway ride up to the top of Mt. San Jacinto more than 8,500 feet in elevation. The tram held 80 people and rotated 360 degrees and as it passed the 5 towers the tram swayed more than slightly and everyone yelled out their surprise. It was funny and scary at the same time. At the station on the top there is a very nice restaurant, a café (where we had lunch), a gift shop and an amazing lookout walk. From there we saw a panorama of the Palm Springs area, the surrounding mountains and the windmill farms (thousands of windmills generate electricity from the wind tunneling through the mountain pass). The camera didn't pick this up too clearly, because we were so high up and it was too far away, but it was incredible to see for miles and miles. It was 80 degrees on the ground and about 50 degrees up top with snow on the mountain.

In Pahrump, Nevada where we camped next to a Winery with free wine tasting everyday and a nice restaurant. For those of you who know me, it doesn't take much for me to feel a little tipsy. so, hey, it was there, it was free and so I decided to taste some wine. I picked one that was a white peak (sweet and fruity) and thought I was getting one taste. Well there were 4 wines in that group and the glass held about 2 mouthfuls per taste; that's 8 mouthfuls of wine, so yes, you guessed it, I got a good buzz and was giggling at anything. It was a really fun time for everyone at the bar. I'm sure they'll remember this Jersey Girl. Death Valley is only about 10 miles from where we camped in Nevada, but it is 98% over the border in California. I didn't realize it was so big (the second largest National Park in the USA, one in Alaska being the first), nor so mountainous. We spent 8 hours traveling over 225 miles and saw maybe only 1/3 of it, but we saw most of the highlights. We took some off road trips that were dirty, dusty, bumpy, and slow going and I don't really know why we took them. We saw the Borax museum. Remember the 20-mule team commercial on TV? Actually it was 18 mules and 2 horses. How these people lived here is beyond me. Well, some didn't make it and over 100 died trying to find a shortcut to the gold mines of central California. That's why it's called Death Valley. One of the most incredible attractions was the Artist's Drive road. It had amazing rock formations in beautiful colors, like aqua green and coral. The Bad Water Basin was also awesome at 282 feet below sea level. It is the lowest point in the Continental US.

On the mountain behind us was a sign that read Sea Level. It was amazing how far up it was. In fact, you can barely find the sign in our picture, so I didn't include it. I think this was the first time we were under sea level without getting wet. We had to stay on the boardwalk that covered the basin because some kind of crustations lived under the salt formations. In the distance is Telescope Peak that is over 11,000 feet above sea level. Incredible.
Love to all,
Renee' & Pete

APR 2 2009

BADWATER BASIN
282 FEET / 855 METERS
BELOW SEA LEVEL

APR 6

APR 8 2009

18

May 16, 2009

Hi Everyone,

On the way to Arches National Park, the scenery was incredible with mountains, canyons, and a vast vista of zero inhabitation. We had to stop to take movies to try to capture the awesomeness of it. It was a wonderful drive full of surprising rock formations and amazing colors, not to mention the color of the deep blue sky. The temperatures at Arches were in the high 80's and down to the low 50's at night. We had to hike 1 ½ miles up and down hills on a dirt path to see Landscape Arch and I had to stop a few times to catch my breath. I was sweaty, dirty and gritty by the time we got there and stopped as soon as we could take a picture. It was like "OK, there it is, let's go". But the next arch was amazing. We only had to hike a few hundred feet and had to squeeze between boulders to get to the site and I thought, "How did they find this place?" It was nice and cool in the shade of the boulders and that's Pete standing under the arch waving. One of the rock formations looked like an elephant. The Balancing Rock is huge and it's just not possible that it doesn't fall over. I wish we could have gotten closer to the world famous Delicate Arch, but we were just too tired to hike there late in the afternoon. It is amazing to see the vastness of the rock formation called Park Avenue, and the rocks appear so thin. Why don't they fall over? We saw a huge formation called the Courthouse and the Tower of Babel is close by. We saw Three Gossips, Pothole Arch, Windows and Turret Arch and the Petrified Sand Dunes. There are over 2,000 arches. There were so many miles and miles of "wows". It took us 2 days to see some of it.

Love to all,

Renee' & Pete

June 9, 2009

Hi Everyone,

Mt. Rushmore is such a patriotic place we could almost feel the American spirit of Freedom. When we walked down the concourse, we can see the flags from every state and on granite pillars are the names of each state, what number it was when it entered the Union and the date. Did you know that New Jersey was the 3rd state? Bet you don't know the first! Now I do. There is a museum there that shows each stage of the carving and how 90% of it was blasted with dynamite and to think it was done in the 1930's is just incredible, because I didn't know it was even invented back then. How did they know where to put those sticks of dynamite? The museum showed all about the sculptor who worked on it for 14 years but didn't live to see the final dedication. It had to be completed by his son Lincoln who led a crew of hundreds of men. The way the sculptor and his workers hoisted themselves all over that mountain is mind-boggling. Washington's nose is twice the height of a single man. Whew! We learned all about the Presidents and why they were chosen for the mountain. The models made of the faces before they were carved were made after so much research of every past picture and statue. The face of Lincoln on Mt. Rushmore was modeled after a statue that the sculptor had created himself and is now located in Newark, NJ. It was all so interesting.

We came back another night just to see Mt. Rushmore lit up. They had a lighting ceremony with an outside movie and then a local Boy Scout troop retired the flag. I watched intently to see if they did it right and it brought back memories of me teaching my 2 sons and my other Cub Scouts, Boy Scouts and Webloe Scouts how to do it. At that time the Ranger asked all the military, past or present to come up on the stage and introduce themselves and what branch of service they were in. My Pete went up to witness the lowering of the flag as he is a Viet Nam Vet (I was so proud of him) and it was so nice to see about 25 men there. One little boy was there with a man who was in the service and the boy was representing his mother who was in the army and not there. By the way Mt. Rushmore got its name from a lawyer, Charles Rushmore, who kept asking his guide the name of all the mountains. The guide got frustrated by all the questions and said, "I don't know, call it Mt. Rushmore". And it stuck

The day we went to see Mt. Rushmore we also went to Custer State Park. It was a zigzagging two lane paved road that turned into a one-lane road in some spots. Before we entered a tunnel, we had to beep our horn so that the vehicle on the other side would stop and let us go through. There were about 6 tunnels, all too small for the motor home to fit through and at one tunnel, the other car didn't beep his horn. He was nice enough to back out of the tunnel and let us come through. There is a road called Needles Highway because the rock formations look like darning needles. In fact, one of the formations is called the Needles Eye. I couldn't get the top of the Eye in my picture because it was so big. It took only about 1-½ hours to travel through the Park. From there we went to see the sculpture of Crazy Horse. It was carved by one of the assistant sculptors of Mt. Rushmore. It is not completed. This man also died before it was done, but now 5 of his 10 children are working to finish it. It was started 63 years ago and relies on donations and the income from the entrance fees and gift shops to finance it. It was commissioned by all of the Northwest Indian Nations to show that they had their own heroes too. There is a museum there with artifacts from all over the Northwest of jewelry, moccasins, dresses, dolls, tools, statues, tepees, drums, arrowheads, pottery, skins, guns and thousands of pictures. We saw a beautiful pair of gloves worn by Indian Guides that are made from rawhide and each bead is individually hand sewn. The Indians had to dye their beads with berry juice and organic plants. I wouldn't be able to hold those little beads much less have the patience to sew them. It was so incredible seeing all the pictures of the Indians I knew from the western movies, like Sitting Bull, Chief Joseph, Geronimo, Cochise and their squaws, some of them living to be 90 and 100. We ate dinner there (Pete had a buffalo burger) and stayed to watch a laser light show. We were there for hours.

Today we went to the Badlands National Park even though the weather was cloudy, rainy and foggy because we leave tomorrow for Sioux Falls. The Indians call it Lands Bad because it's hard to grow anything. The rock formations are colorful, have holes in them and split with gullies and deep crevices. They look fragile and in fact they do deteriorate about an inch every year. We saw some cars pulled over on the side of the road and saw that they were taking pictures of mountain goats. They were hard to spot because they blend right into the side of the mountain. Look hard at the picture. That is the red tag around the neck of the goat. There were about 6 of them and one was a nursing baby. We also took movies of prairie dogs that look so cute and make a chirping sound. We did not see any rattle snakes as the signs warned, thank God. At the visitor's center we watched a movie about how it was all formed and what animals live there. Sixty million years ago it was all under the great sea that went from the Colorado River to the Mississippi River. After the water went away, Mammoths, Saber Tooth Tigers and 3-toed horses roamed the area. It turned out to be a nice ride and the weather even got a little better in the afternoon.

Yesterday we went to the famous Wall Drug Store. It opened in 1931, but didn't do much business with the 300 residents to keep it in business. In 1935 the owner's wife had an idea to put up signs by the road telling travelers to come in for a free glass of ice water. (In 1935 where did they get the ice from in the summer? Did they have freezers then? I don't think so. Pete said they froze water in the winter and saved it for the summer. Really?) After that, they couldn't keep up with the customers and had to hire 8 girls to help out. Now they have expanded to a whole city block and carries not only drugs and personal items, but it also has a soda fountain with homemade ice cream, root beer floats, free donuts and coffee for Military and Vets, homemade fudge and candy and a restaurant. It stocks western shirts, boots, leather gloves, cowboy hats, souvenirs, camping gear and has an art store, book store, candy store and a chapel. The back is for kids with an arcade, a dinosaur that roars and snarls smoke with flashing lights, more shops and a water amusement that spouts jets of water from the ground. It was fun watching this one little boy of about 2 years old rush from one spout to another and screaming and laughing. We were laughing hysterically ourselves.
Love to All,
Renee' & Pete

July 21, 2010

Hi Everyone,

We are camped right in the Theodore Roosevelt National Park for 4 nights. No electric (except for our generator which we are only allowed to run during the day), and no water hookups. We are dry-docking. It is in the high 70's during the day and 50's at night. Outside of the visitor's center we saw lots of people looking over a stone wall. When we walked up to the wall we saw a landscape full of pink tipped hills and a vista that went as far as the eye could see. We didn't even have a clue this was there from the road. The view was incredible.

Theodore Roosevelt loved to hunt and ride his horse around the beautiful country and his log cabin (built in 1883) is here behind the visitor's center. His house has 1 bedroom, a kitchen and living room. No bathroom. Hum? In his lifetime he wrote 3-dozen books and read one to three books a day. While he was visiting here on Valentine's Day he received word that his wife died 2 days after giving birth to a baby girl and his mother, who had typhoid, died on the same day. They lived in the same house in New York City. He was devastated and depressed. He was also part owner of a cattle ranch in 1884-1887 when he was only 27, until an unusually bad winter killed 75% of the stock. He sold the ranch and went into politics. He wanted to preserve the beautiful land and animals and proclaimed some territories National Parks during his term as President, but this Park was dedicated to him in the 1950's after his death at the age of 60. The Teddy Bear was also created in his honor

We just got back from riding around the Park on a road that loops around the middle of it. Even though I just saw it, it is hard to describe. It is mostly stark mountains, some of which are bare and we can see the lines and different colors of sedimentary rocks that represent different stages of time from the ice age glaciers to the volcanic debris from the West, deposited here thousands of years ago. Some of the mountains are covered in green trees and grass. As we drive around a curve the scenery is more breathtaking than the last. We have seen wild horses and lots of prairie dog meadows that house thousands of the little critters. It was so much fun trying to capture them on camera, trying to time the picture so that I got them sitting up before they scurried in their little mound home. They make a high-pitched sound almost like a baby's squeeze toy. They look like a big hamster or a gerble. I could watch them for hours. As we rounded the turn we saw a huge bison bull just walking there on the side of the road. We were afraid to pass him because he was so close and as we did he turned his head to look at us and I was praying he wouldn't charge. A guy riding a bike was stopped in the other direction and he was contemplating whether to pass him or not. Ultimately, he waited for a car to come along and he rode on the passenger side on the shoulder for protection. Whew! That was scary.

September 15, 2010
Hi Everyone
On 9/2 we took a ferry ride from Anacortes, WA to Friday Harbor in the San Juan Islands. We didn't take the car and just walked onto the ferry and backpacked it. It was a beautiful day with lots of sunshine and the ferry was quite big with comfortable seats and lots of windows (not too clean). The water was calm and except for the movement of the boat, we did not notice any rocking. On the way over we saw a harbor seal with a salmon in his mouth. One minute he was there and the next he was gone so fast we couldn't even get a picture. The mountains in the distance and the boats in the harbors reminded me of our cruise to Alaska, very picturesque. When we got to Friday Harbor we walked off the ferry and into a cute little seaport town with lots of shops and restaurants and right across the street was a shuttle bus to take us to Lime Kiln Point so that we could go Orca whale watching. Orca whales are the huge black and white ones like Shamoo, the one in Seaworld. In the picture of the lighthouse, we sat on those boulders that were jutting out beyond the point to watch the whales. It was very uncomfortable. We were around that area for about 4 hours, just walking and climbing the boulders. We were told that the whales come as close as 50 feet from the shore, but that day they were about a mile away. I saw some of them blowing the water from their blowholes and I did see some of the dorsal fins with the binoculars. They were probably showing off for the dozen tour boats waiting for the whales and I'm sure they were able to get much closer. I thought we would have more fun exploring the lookout point and we did.

 It wasn't just the whale watching, it was also the lighthouse that was there that attracted us, but we were not able to go inside. It is automatically operated now. It is advertised that there are 3 pods of Orcas that go past that point everyday. Each pod has 17 to 50 whales. I don't believe it because I only saw a few and they didn't even jump out of the water. Are they lazy Orcas or was it a tourist trap? On the way back on the ferry we experienced one of the most colorful sunsets we have ever seen. It started out as a few gray clouds with one of the clouds looking like a porpoise with its long bottlenose snout. By the time we arrived at the harbor, the colors were so vivid red and blue, everyone was snapping pictures as we were departing the ferry. It was a perfect picture for a perfect day.
Love to All,
Renee' & Pete

On September 4th we went to Mt. Rainier National Park. It is very beautiful country. Just after we passed the Ranger Station we stopped the car and walked down a small inclined path to see Christine Falls. I am standing on a deck overlooking the stream with the falls in the background, but above the falls is the stone bridge that we had just crossed over. So what's the big attraction? Mt. Rainier is a snowcapped volcano 14,410 feet high and the tallest peak of the Cascade Range. As the road twists and turns around the volcano and through the Park, it peaks in and out of view so we saw it from all sides. The surrounding mountains are covered with huge evergreen trees. We spent 6 hours driving around its 235,000 acres and we never got tired of seeing the grandeur of this one mountain (volcano). A naturalist named it Paradise. So that's the big attraction. I'm glad we went.

Next we visited Mt. St. Helens National Park. Pete and we were awe-struck by the stark devastation of this area. Do you remember how long ago it erupted? Pete thought it was only 5 or 10 years ago and I thought it was in the 1990's. Do you believe it was in May 1980? The forest was cleared and 90% of it has been replanted, an area of 250 sq. miles that has grown back to become mature evergreen trees. A huge portion of the destroyed area was left untouched as a reminder of this catastrophe. When we went to the Forest Learning Center, we saw how the area looked before the eruption. Then we saw a re-enactment of the explosion in a 4-minute video complete with incredible sound. It was like 2,000 atomic bombs going off that sent 540,000 tons of ash rocketing into the stratosphere. Ash was measurable more than 900 miles to the east and trace amounts circled the Earth in 10 days. As we traveled along the road to Mt. St. Helens, we stopped at a few lookout points to see the devastation that the lava flow and the lahars caused, miles and miles before we even saw the volcano. At the time of the explosion, the mountain had snow on it and it all melted instantly. Add to that the lava, the trees, and rocks and it all enters the river with a force that causes a tidal wave and all the houses and trees and bridges are washed away in minutes. The boulders and the moving lava score the earth and it looks like a giant animal has pawed the earth. It is very fascinating.

Clouds were circling the side crater and steam still emits from the sleeping giant so it was hard to get a clear picture. At the Visitor's Center we saw another movie of the eruption, not as powerful as the first, and at the end of the movie we watched as the screen was raised and Mt. St. Helens was seen beyond the huge observation window. It was quite impressive. After the movie we exited to an information area that presented pictures and eyewitness accounts by some of the area residents and survivors. Over 100 people died.

In the museum, Pete was standing next to part of a gray tree that was blown sideways by the force of the explosion and the top of the tree was parallel along the ceiling and looked like giant toothpicks still attached to the stump. Outside, all around us are thousands of dead trees that are gray and lying on the ground, but they were propelled through the air and spiral marks can be seen scored into their bark by the debris and boulders twirling around with them. Part of the mountain directly across from Mt. St. Helens was blown away from the force. It is all so mind-boggling. We were very sad as we left the park, but very happy that most of it is thriving again thanks to Weyerhaeuser Lumber Company and thousands of volunteers who painstakingly replanted most of the trees. Now all the trees are the same age, the same height and as you look at the surrounding mountains, the trees look like they are in 3D and played tricks with our eyes.

September 26, 2010

Traveling along the coast of Oregon is kind of scary, especially in a 40 ft. motor home and towing a SUV. Mostly the road is along a cliff and the drop is long and rocky. In fact, we could see huge boulders way out beyond the shoreline sticking out of the water and it seems odd that they are there at all. We encountered some bridges going over water as usual, but some of the bridges are cut into the side of the mountains. In Newport the condos go right up to the beach which is bumpy and not a smooth surface like NJ. We watched the waves and the sunset and were rewarded with a spectacular site. Once the sun reaches the water it looks like a fireball and it sets within a minute. Here, the sun sets directly into the Pacific. West Coast people love their sunsets like we love our sunrises. We used to drive onto Island Beach State Park, actively fished all night by our bonfire and just waited for the beautiful sunrise.

Oh, get this. If you can see the beach you are in a Tsunami Zone and there are evacuation route signs all along the way. This is new for us and a little daunting. There are two kinds of Tsunamis. There are foreign Tsunamis (which give you about 1 hour's notice by sirens to get to safety and the waves are 25+ feet high), and there are local Tsunamis, which are only 8+ feet high. They're just as scary because you have only minutes to escape it. I was a little on edge all the while we camped there, but the local residents seem to take it all in stride. We took note of the escape route, just in case.

Finally, we got to the Redwood National Park. Ok, so it was like driving through a forest, only this forest had trees 3 times the height of those in NJ and is pretty wide around its base. The main road through it is only about 18 miles long and it took us about ½ hour. We stopped at a visitor's center and figured we would go back to the campground, there's nothing else. There were a few trails, but we don't hike. Then, I read that there was a scenic dirt road with some streams and we might see some wildlife. We had some time to kill, we had 4-wheel drive so, let's go there. On the way, we saw about 5 cars pulled over on the side of the road. It could only mean one thing. Wildlife is close. We see a herd of elk and hope that is not all we see. We start off on the dirt road and it is like going on a rocky roller coaster. We are not only being thrown from side to side, but the bumps are making our teeth chatter and we are only going 5 mph. How long is this road? It's dark in here, narrow and we are the only car on this road. Hello, AAA? Ok, I spoke too soon. Here comes a car! One of us has to decide to pull over to the side. That was nice of them to do it. Our son Mike would've loved this road with his ATV. There are huge Redwood trees here too and it seemed like miles before we see daylight and the Ocean peaking through the trees.

The first and second streams are only a trickle of water to cross, but the third is a quarter way up the tires and the fourth is about halfway. Not too bad. (The Weather Channel says two foot of water can float a pickup. Uh Oh!) I hung out the window to take movies of the crossing. Awesome! We got to the end of the road at a parking lot and we can walk a path to the beach. We declined. Nothing's exciting and it's about 5:00 now so we decide to head back before that road really gets dark. I told Pete to stop as we crested a hill so I could take a picture of the beach and holy crow, there in the distance is an elk bull just hanging out by himself. We can only see his head and we didn't know if it was standing or sitting in the tall grass. We watched him for about 5 minutes but he didn't move. We start to go again and coming up the road are two more elk. The road is narrow here and one walks past Pete and he could almost put his hand out the window and touch him if he didn't want his hand anymore. We are always reminded that these animals are wild and we should not get too close to them or feed them. No worry there for me. As the other elk walks past my side, Pete rolls down my window and the elk looked right at me. I almost jumped into Pete's lap and yelled repeatedly for him not to stop the car in very loud whispers. My heart was in my throat because if the elk turned his head slightly it would be in the car window. I hit Pete because he was laughing at me.

We drive on a few feet more and here's a huge bull elk, about 1,200 pounds with 6 female elk (don't know what they are called) and 3 young buck elk. The bull is protecting his girls and he's chasing 2 of the bucks but they run a short distance and wander back like "nah nah da nah nah". The other is by himself acting very unassuming. We watched them for about 45 minutes. This was so exciting because they came so close to us and every once in a while the bull elk would look our way to make sure we stayed where we were. We didn't make any sudden moves and we talked in whispers. Pete stood on the running board of the car and placed the movie camera on the roof to steady it. We got really good movies. The elk were still there when we left. They made the whole day worthwhile.

October 16, 2010

Today we went to San Francisco. It was another beautiful day and on the way to the Golden Gate Bridge we passed Lombard Street. We found it by accident and when we finally got to the top I was so awestruck I forgot to take a picture of it, but I did take movies. It was really incredible and took my breath away. I'm not just talking about the outstanding view of San Francisco Bay, but the structure of the street. It is a zigzag formation. Picture the width of a two-lane road, but this is only one-way; down. While we maneuvered from one side of the street to the other and around 2 ft. walls topped with beautiful flowers of every kind, we are going down a very, very steep incline at 5 mph. It takes only about three minutes. I think the walls are there in case we tip over. In the meantime there are pretty two-story townhouses built together and declining in height as we traversed the hill. The sidewalk is a series of stairs and landings that I couldn't possibly climb if I had to or would I want to and yet here are crowds of people coming and going as if it was a mission and a piece of cake. Whew! Kudos to them.

It was Fleet Week in San Francisco and not only were there tons of boats on the Bay, but the Blue Angles were putting on a show by the Golden Gate Bridge and Fisherman's Warf. There must have been 100,000 people in the area and that means traffic and hard to find parking spaces. As we got to the Golden Gate Bridge Park, Blue Angles were flying overhead and I jumped out of my skin when one of them broke the sound barrier and a sonic boom passed through my body. Car alarms started sounding all around us and we laughed at the noise and the shear fun of it. Picture the blue sky, the blue water with white sailboats, the magnificence of the red (or golden) bridge and the mountains in the distance. It was awesome and we couldn't believe we were there. I was taking a picture of Pete when a male jogger stopped and asked if we wanted him to take our picture. That was nice of him and I told him I didn't want to interrupt his jog. He said he was a Marine and that was his mission for the day. This is the picture that he took. I thanked him for his help and his service and told him Pete was a Viet Nam vet. They shook hands and with pats on the shoulders he turned and jogged away. Isn't this a great Country? The comradeship brought tears to my eyes. Of course, we just had to go across the bridge and we briefly saw Sausalito on the other side before we turned around and came back. We were on our way to Pier 39 off of Fisherman's Wharf.

As we were walking along the wharf and pier we stopped to watch the Blue Angles perform again. Watching them just gave us goose bumps as they soared past each other and paint objects in the sky with their red white and blue exhaust. Their formation seems so close that just a tiny miscalculation could cause a catastrophe. We thoroughly enjoyed watching them, especially since Pete was in the Air Force. After the show we continued to the back of the pier and saw Alcatraz Island in the distance as all the boats passed to and fro across the Bay. Pier 39 juts out into the San Francisco Bay and is about a quarter mile long. It has a docking area for tour boats and a boardwalk on one side with a row of two story shops and restaurants and entertainment in the center complete with a stage, a carousel, kiddy rides and vender stalls in the middle. There is another row of shops and restaurants on the other side too, complete with Bubba Gump Shrimp Co. (from the movie "Forest Gump") and a band played near the exit. There are 300 sea lions that live there all year round and came there after the 1989 San Francisco earthquake. They smell and fight and crawl all over each other as they lazily bask in the California sun.

November 7, 2010

We met Mike at the Sacramento airport and it was so good to see him. I can't believe he packed everything (including his computer) into a backpack. When he got into the car it was nonstop talking. After we had lunch in our motor home we went shopping to a Raider's Image store close by and we just had to go there and buy hats for the Raider's game on Sunday. Joe didn't get off of work until late and it was finally so nice to see Mike & Joe together. We hadn't seen Mike since July and Joe hadn't seen him since Christmas. We are very blessed that we love each other so much and have so much fun together. It's nice that we are all adults and that the awkward growing up period is behind us. It's like we're all buddies. The guys were kidding each other about sleeping together on the pullout couch and all of a sudden Joe called out "I'm the big spoon", Mike just groaned and we all laughed until our sides split. We just knew the weekend was going to be good. When Joe got off of work, we left at 4:30 to go to San Francisco again. It took about 1 ½ hours and by the time we went over the Golden Gate Bridge from the Sausalito side the sun was starting to set. Mike just about had time to see the bridge and the Bay and we rushed to get to Bakers Beach so he could put his hands in the San Francisco Bay. The view of the bridge was awesome and we were rewarded again with a magnificent California sunset. From there, we just had to show Mike Lombard St. On the way there, we went up a really steep street and the car in front of us disappeared as it crested the hill and went down the other side. It was like a roller coaster ride and we were all yelling as we went over the top. So cool.

Il suggested we go to Bubba Gump Shrimp Co. for dinner since we had missed it the last time we were here and Mike could see Pier 39, Fisherman's Wharf and the sea lions. When we walked into the restaurant, Forest Gump the movie was playing continuously and we could buy T Shirts that read "Stupid is as Stupid Does" and "Life is like a box of Chocolates". Our Filipino waitress reminded me of Joan a little and she smiled when Joe spoke a little of the Tagalla language to her. She was asking us trivia questions while we waited for our food and was surprised when we knew most of the answers. Then we quizzed her and when she missed one of them we cheered. There was a sign on the end of the table that reads Run Forrest Run. If we needed a waitress, we could flip it to Stop Forrest Stop and any waiter or waitress would come right to our table. After a really tasty meal I was surprised when all of the servers stopped at our table and everyone in the restaurant sang Happy Birthday to me. It was hard for me not to cry. Boy, I didn't realize how long that song is. Outside of the restaurant, Pete was pretending to be Forrest Gump with his feet inside Forrest's sneakers and his suitcase and box of chocolates was by his side. We had an incredible day.

We decided to stay at a hotel for the night so we could be close to the Raider's Coliseum and get there early. So, in the morning, after Joe and Mike went for a run and we met for breakfast in the lobby, we quickly packed up and went to the game. It was Halloween and we saw lots of costumes, mostly pirates, and lots of black Raider's jerseys. There were thousands of tailgaters and all we could smell is lighter fluid, charcoal, hamburgers, hot dogs, sausage and anything else that was tossed on the grills, yum. Some people went all out and cooked lobster, clams and steak. We took a walk around and someone had an ice sculpture with the Raider's logo on it. There was a cup at the top and a tube going through it. When they mixed their drink they poured it in the top and it would get cold as it traveled through the ice and they would drink it on the bottom from a tube. The Raider's slogan is "Raider Nation" and Bud Light's slogan is "One Beer, One Nation". Mike brought us his collection of Raider's shirts to wear. We didn't even wear the winter hats that we bought because we were on the sunny side of the stadium and we roasted in the sun with not a cloud in the sky. It was probably 85 degrees and we could have worn bathing suits. Thanks to the man sitting in front of us who shared his sun block lotion with us or else Joe and I would have been burned to a crisp. Wearing Raider's black shirts didn't help either. We all commented that the field looked so small compared to the TV and it was just so exciting when the cheerleaders and players came onto the field that it brought tears to my eyes because we were all actually there. Our seats were on the Seahawks side and we had our choice of seats because it wasn't crowded there on the 30-yard line just below the box seats and close to the field. The game was very exciting too. Raider's won 33 to 3. Mike was on cloud nine. AWESOME!!!!!

When we got back to Sacramento, we went to the Red Lobster (my favorite restaurant) and everyone sang Happy Birthday to me again. We were so exhausted by the time we got back to the motor home that we were all sleeping by 9:30. In the morning Mike and Joe woke us up to say goodbye with big hugs and kisses. Joe was taking Mike to the airport at 6:15 to get his plane at 7:30 and Joe was going to work. We were surprised again when Joe came back at night to eat a quick dinner with us before he caught his plane at 7:30 pm. Yeah! More hugs & kisses. Boo! We won't see them until maybe June because we decided not to go home for Christmas. Travel expenses are just too high.Life is so good when you can have fabulous weekends like this and I wish this for everyone. Too bad they go so fast, but I think we squeezed every happy minute into it. Thanks Joe for arranging everything and for sharing your frequent flyer miles with Mike and making a dream come true for all of us. It was the best Birthday weekend with my sons ever!

March 4, 2011

Pete and I just got back from an incredible 2-week stay in Kuaii (sounds like Hawaii with a K instead of an H). Everything went well except for 2 things. I lost one of my favorite white gold earrings on a rough catamaran ride and I also lost my camera on the way home, probably at the airport. That's right; all my pictures of the second week are gone. Pete downloaded the first week's pictures into the computer, so I have those, thank God. Eileen said she will send me a CD of her pictures. I am so heartbroken because you know how much I love to take pictures of everything. Oh well, we'll get another.

We met my sister Eileen and her husband Steve at the LA airport and traveled together to the last island of the Hawaiian chain of islands. They live in Minnesota and were happy to get away from the snow. Eileen & I were given beautiful purple and white leis of real flowers when we checked in at the condo and Pete and Steve were given pretty beaded leis. Our condo had two bedrooms with our own baths, a living room/dining room combo, a small kitchenette with modern appliances and granite countertops and a covered deck. All the rooms had ceiling fans and the windows were all open. It was in the high 80's with 98% humidity during the day and it was still hot in the rooms because there were no air conditioners. It was hard to sleep because of that and because I was still so pumped about being there.

The next morning when I got up, I walked out onto the deck and walked into a tropical paradise. The palm trees & palm bushes were all full and still. Where are the tropical trade winds that are supposed to cool me instead of air conditioning? Everything was very lush and green with beautifully colored flowers, like huge hydrangeas of yellows, pinks and reds and there were so many other flowers I don't know the names of. The 400 inches of rain a year on this island water the plants and it looks like the plants and trees just suck it all up. The weather was so humid and hot my hair was instantly curly and frizzy and every surface felt damp to the touch. But who cares, I'm in Hawaii.

Hanalei Bay is very popular for surfing, snorkeling, swimming and there is a long pier for fishing. The pier was built in 1892 to aid local farmers to ship their produce. Do you remember the song "Puff the Magic Dragon"? It was created here and inspired by the mountains in the distance that were supposed to look like a dragon to the author. We really had to use our imagination to even remotely picture a dragon.

43

Getting back in the car we traversed over one-lane bridges and a narrow twisting country road to get to the tunnel beaches. On one side of the road is a mountain with a tunnel underneath it. I'm glad I'm the one taking the pictures because I'm not going anywhere close to that cave. It was dark in there with stuff hanging down from the ceiling and it was damp. The walls and ceiling are black lava and the floor is sand, so the ocean probably cut this tunnel after a volcano eruption That is hard to believe because the ocean is across the street and a long distance from the tunnel. Maybe a tsunami created it. There are tsunami sirens at every beach and bay, which is kind of scary. I took a picture of the lifeguard station. It's a little metal hut on stilts with windows all around and I wonder if it's air-conditioned.

The next day we took a tour by van, plane and boat. The van guide was very knowledgeable and also very funny. He took us through a neighborhood close to the Princeville Cliffs where we were staying and showed us some albatross birds and their nests. Did you know that the albatross can travel great distances and they are the only bird that drinks seawater? The albatross was that goofy bird in "The Little Mermaid". They actually look like that too. The houses were pretty nice. Can you imagine having an albatross nest on your lawn? The residents didn't seem to mind.

The first stop was to the airport to catch a small tour plane for a tour of the island. Steve told us that he got sick last year after the ride and didn't want to go. Hearing that, I decided not to go and to keep him company. Pete was in the Air Force so he was really eager to go and Eileen enjoyed it last year, so she wanted to go too. I had the camera, so Pete took pictures with his cell phone. They came out pretty good. The first aerial photo is of the Waimea Canyon that is like a mini Grand Canyon. My pictures of it are still in my camera that I lost and I'm so happy that Pete took so many pictures. I hope you can get an idea of how deep it is. We visited it by car the second week we were there and it was very cold, rainy and windy plus we traveled up about 4,000 feet to the lookout points. The views were breathtaking and the wind just took my breath away. The second aerial photo was of the Wailua Falls. It was so interesting to compare Pete's aerial photos with our land photos. The falls are about as tall as the Niagara Falls, but not as wide. I think the Guide said they were 75 feet high. While Pete & Eileen were on the plane the Guide took Steve and I to a few places. I took my picture of the falls from a bridge that goes right past it, but I didn't get to see as much of the surrounding area as Pete did. The Guide told us about a lot of movies and TV shows that were filmed there and "Jurassic Park" is one of them. "South Pacific" with Mitzy Gaynor is another one. Steve and I visited a place where "Donovan's Reef" was filmed in the 60's maybe?

45

OK, so back to the airport to pick up Eileen and Pete and they don't even have time to go to the bathroom and we are whisked away in the van and taken to the dock for a boat ride up the Wailua River and State Park where we walk through a rain forest to a fern grotto.Guitar players and a few hula dancers accompanied us to perform a story about past couples that got married there and found happiness and good luck. It is a beautiful spot with the bright green trees and vibrant red flowers that are made into leis. There were bananas growing on the tree above our heads. The leaves are huge!

Pete and Eileen flew over the Kilauea Lighthouse and later the Guide drove us there. We spent about an hour watching whales in the distance. Mostly we could only see the blow spray, but there were a lot of them. We left our binoculars in the van. We did see some seals on a mound of rocks just below the lighthouse and a huge tortoise swimming by. It was also very windy. The top of the lighthouse is covered with black cloth while they are making repairs. To the right of this cliff is another cliff that is a refuge for thousands of Red Legged birds like seagulls.

We took an ill-fated catamaran ride to the Na Pali Coast. It was sunny when we started out and Eileen, Steve and I took Dramamine pills just to be sure. About an hour out we started to get rough seas and rain, but I was still able to get some fabulous pictures of whales. I got 2 pictures (not shown here) of the tales of the whales going back into the water, but they were too far away. They look great when I zoomed in before printing. I also got a picture of a whale doing a back flip and I can't believe I got it! I was so proud. The tour then took us to the Na Pali coast where huge mountains drop into the ocean. We cannot drive to this part of the Island and can only see it by boat or plane. Pete took this picture from the plane. It was amazing. There was an incredible arch formed by the waves in the side of the mountain and the rain hindered the view from the boat. Most of the mountains were covered with clouds, which only made it more awesome to see. The first mate took the front cover picture of Pete and I when the sun came out briefly and it was really windy. We then had a light dinner of salads and Teriyaki Chicken and some type of London broil served in onions and mushrooms. That's when my sister lost it. (Sorry Eileen I have to tell the story). She vomited in her plate and thank God Pete was sitting next to her and not me because he casually shoved his plate in front of her when her plate got full of vomit. I would have froze and been no help. Then the first mate came over with a bag and escorted her to the back of the boat and instructed her to project any forthcoming vomit over the back of the boat. He was very helpful. She was not alone, there were 4 other women there too.

47

The second week we went to a really nice souvenir shop called Hilo Hatties in Lihue. As we entered the shop, we were given beaded leis and a cup of coffee or juice. They had really beautiful Hawaiian shirts and I bought a pretty dress and lots of souvenirs. When we left we were given a free sarong. We even went back another day to buy more stuff. I love this store. Afterwards, we went to a real Lu'au and show. They roasted a pig (pigs run wild on the island) and I was disappointed that it was served as pulled pork when I was expecting a nice piece of sliced pork or pork chop. It was a buffet with other food and salads including Teriyaki Chicken. (Chickens also run wild on the island, hmmmm). It was OK, but the show was spectacular. Lots of Hula dancing and fire torches telling the story of how the Polynesian people came to the island. We had front row seats, but we weren't allowed to take pictures. I took lots of pictures of the hula dancers and actors afterward, but they are in the lost camera. We really enjoyed it.

The next day we went to see the Spouting Horn in Koloa. The ocean waves slide under a shelf of lava rocks and when pressure mounts up it spouts out through the holes above. They can spout 20 to 30 feet in the air. It was fun trying to time the big spouts and take a picture. They had kiosks of hand made beads, purses, clothes and jewelry. The perpetual roosters were there too. Wherever we went on the island beautiful roosters and chickens were there. There were actually mobs of them. I loved taking their pictures because they were so colorful. From there we went to a dinner show of South Pacific. I loved all the old songs by Rogers and Hammerstein like "There Ain't Nothing Like a Dame", "Some Enchanted Evening", "Bali Hai", "I'm Gonna Wash That Man Right Out of My Hair" and so many others. The acting was very, very good.

We also took a trip to the local coffee plantation in Eleele, but stayed mostly in the gift shop where they gave out samples of their coffee, which, of course we were able to buy for $14 a pound. I also bought coconut syrup to bring back home with us (can't wait to make pancakes). We didn't take the tour because it was raining, but it was interesting to learn all about it.

Well that's about it. We had a fabulous time that went very quickly. We were busy almost everyday and Eileen and Steve are very generous hosts.

Love to all,

Renee' and Pete

Photo Creations

51